MONEY MAGIC

Clearing Your Path To Money, Time And Happiness

Michelle Masters

Money Magic
Copyright ©2018 Michelle Masters

All Rights Reserved. Printed in the U.S.A.
ISBN-13: 978-1729496244

All rights reserved. No part of this book may be reproduced or used in any manner without written permission of the copyright owner except for the use of quotations in a book review.

The events and conversations in this book have been set down to the best of the author's ability, although some names and details have been changed to protect the privacy of individuals.

Big Disclaimer

This work is solely for personal growth, inspiration and entertainment. It is not psychotherapy or counseling, and in no way should be treated as a substitute for licensed, professional assistance. Using the change patterns or information in this book is the choice of the reader, who assumes full responsibility for his or her understandings, experiences and results. The author and publisher assume no responsibility for the actions or choices of any reader.

(Always a good policy in life. Yay, free will!)

Book design by Epic Author Publishing

Contact: 800-273-1625 | support@epicauthor.com | EpicAuthor.com

For Denny

PLEASE JOIN US AT ONE OF OUR
WORKSHOPS, EITHER LIVE, OR ONLINE.
TO FIND OUT ABOUT OUR WORKSHOPS GO TO:

http://www.michellemastersnlp.com

TABLE OF CONTENTS

Introduction   1

How to Use This Book   5

ONE: The Call
Or, When Your Life Changes in a
Staff Meeting and You Don't Even Know It   9

TWO: How Your Three Brains Make or Cost You Money
Or, Why You Don't Already Have What You Want   15

THREE: The Life-changing Question
Or, Your Compass for Life and Money   25

FOUR: The Glasses You Don't Know You Are Wearing
Or, How to Spot Your Core Beliefs   37

FIVE: The Invisible Ceiling
Or, Money, Worth and Deserving   53

SIX: What's in Your Personals Ad?
Or, Your Relationship to Money   61

SEVEN: The Biggest Block to Everything You Want
Or, God Must Really Love Rap Musicians   69

EIGHT: The Death of the Zero Sum
Or, How Many Jelly Beans in the Universal Jar?   81

NINE: You Walk in Magic
Or, Your Greatest Symphony of All Want More Magic?   87

Acknowledgments   95

About the Author   99

Introduction

"Have fun storming the castle!
—Miracle Max from The Princess Bride

In my early 20s, I was living in New York on almost no money. My room had been the laundry room of an old Brooklyn apartment. It was so narrow that I had to roll my small futon up every morning because it occupied almost the entire room. I can manage a fairly spartan existence, but eventually, when I had to keep turning down invitations to go out or do anything that cost money, it finally got to me. A friend from my softball team called and asked if I wanted to go out to dinner. Going out to dinner meant that I would have no money left for food for the rest of the week, and I am very much in favor of eating—but I was fed up with living that way, so after an intense inner battle, I said yes. When the subject of ordering dessert came up the fear rose again, but I thought, *no. I am not going to live my life in fear of not having enough money.* Dessert was on.

As we finished dessert, the worlds' tiniest cockroach (and I do mean tiny—a ladybug would be considered serious muscle in comparison) ran across our table. My friend panicked and frantically swatted at the table. She had no better hand/eye coordination when it came to cockroach swatting than she did at softball, though, so all she was doing was making the silverware fly. I wasn't worried because: a) it was New York, and all the buildings have cockroaches, and b) unlike some New York cockroaches I was pretty sure I could take this one in a fight, but my friend was making a scene. So, I reached over and gently took care of it with my napkin. Then, I looked for a trash can to put it in, but because this was a restaurant and not a fast food joint, there weren't trash cans all around. A waitress saw me looking around and asked if I needed help, so I told her what had happened, and she offered to take the napkin and presumably give the cockroach a decent burial.

As you can probably guess when we asked for the bill the waitress told us it was on the house because of our deceased little friend. It may seem a small thing, but I will never forget the feeling that **when you make a decision about how you want to live your life; the universe will move with you.** It has stayed with me all these years. I have had bigger and flashier examples of that since then, but maybe none as important—because that event in New York—when I stood in my laundry/bedroom and decided to say yes to an invitation—was the first time I took control over how I wanted to create my life.

I had to learn that lesson a few more times, but most importantly, I had to learn the tools that would allow me to *change the patterns* that were in the way.

Changing your patterns is what this book is for. It contains stories, insights and some of the exercises from my Money Magic workshop that will help you to *change the patterns that are in your way.*

Unless you change the patterns that are in your way (almost all of which are subconscious), you will always be fighting yourself and the world. Once your patterns change, however, the wind is at your back, and the world is at your feet. Things move more easily. Opportunities show up. Chance meetings with just the right people start happening.

Life gets easier and richer—in every sense.

How to Use this Book

The insights and stories in this book communicate to different parts of your brain—our policy is always to leave no brain hemisphere behind—so it's suggested that you **read it all**.

At the end of some of the chapters are change patterns. These are exercises that will begin to rewire your neurology to have and create more of what you want, and less of what you don't want. The change patterns *revise the internal software* you have running that is in the way of having what you want. The change patterns are what sets Money Magic apart from most other work. Understanding what's in your way is wonderful, but understanding won't change the patterning—just like understanding that it's a reflex to pull your head away when something flies at it, doesn't change the reflex. Deciding that you want to believe something different when you are 35 doesn't change the beliefs that have been running since you were four.

So, the **change patterns are crucial**. These are where the **revisions get made.** Other people wiser than I am have made many of the observations in this book. But unless you change the patterning that is in the way, all the brilliant observations in the world won't make much difference.

So, **do the change patterns**. (Not while you are driving or doing anything where it's not safe to get trancey, and not if you feel unstable—see the Big Disclaimer at the beginning.)

After you have finished reading the book and doing the change patterns, you can go back periodically and do the change patterns again—you can even do them on something else if you like (it doesn't even have to be on the topic of money). Once you have gone through the change patterns, let them integrate for 3-4 weeks or more and see how you feel. If you feel differently, then changes have already started. ***You can look forward to seeing how those positive changes play out.*** If you are still feeling stressed or stuck after 3-4 weeks, you can go back and do the change patterns again, especially on the feeling of being stressed or stuck.

If you want more change, you can always join us at a workshop—either live or online (there are experiences we can facilitate in a workshop that are difficult to translate into a book).

Mostly, I hope you enjoy this book because it should be fun. It should all be fun.

Have fun storming the castle!

CHAPTER ONE

The Call

-OR-

When Your Life Changes in a Staff Meeting and You Don't Even Know It

---

"It's always best to start at the beginning."
—Glinda, the Good Witch of the North in
The Wizard of Oz

J oseph Campbell taught that most adventure stories begin with a Call to Adventure—a message or invitation that starts someone on their way. Harry Potter gets his letter from Hogwarts, R2D2 plays a message for Luke Skywalker, etc.

My call came during a staff meeting at NLP Marin, widely regarded as one of the best training centers in the world in the field of Communication and Change. Our staff meetings, however, were incredibly striking in that, typically, they resulted in neither any communication nor any change.

This meeting, however, was different. (It was not as dramatic as a hologram-projecting droid finding you on your moisture farm and telling you that you are their only hope but still...)

It was 2006, and I was sitting there trying to simultaneously appear relevant and not take up too much space, when our executive director, Denny McGinnis, turned to me and asked if I would be willing to create a 2-day workshop on money. At the time, that was a little like asking a rabbi to create a workshop on 100 different ways to use bacon—because I had zero interest in or knowledge of money.

But I really like creating workshops, so I said yes. And although I knew nothing about money, I did know something about how to create change for people, because that is what we teach, all the time. Carl Buchheit (co-founder of NLP Marin and resident genius) suggested the name Money Magic for the workshop, and without realizing it at the time, something started which I could never have foreseen.

An unexpected adventure had begun.

I still had to create it, though. So, I spent a summer designing a workshop that took the best NLP* change patterns and techniques that I knew and adapted and applied them to the context of money. I also included some of the gifts of Bert Hellinger's Family Constellation work (more on that later). That autumn, we did the first Money Magic workshop, and in the weeks and months afterward, we started receiving lovely reports of all the changes that were showing up for the participants. Incomes had gone up. Unexpected gains and gifts had shown up. People were getting promotions; they were receiving new jobs, new homes, etc.

Then, sometime around 2008, I attended a Matrix Energetics workshop with Richard Bartlett and Melissa Joy. Matrix Energetics provides a way of working in a quantum modality that creates change in stunning, and often immediate ways. When I added in that way of working as well, people started getting changes even *before the workshop began*. People tell me all the time that they register for the workshop and then get a promotion, or an unexpected check in the mail the very next day. By merely registering, they had entered a quantum field of possibilities and collapsed probability waves of what they wanted into their life-often in hard to believe ways (more on that later, too).

Since then, the Money Magic workshop has become its own movement. Between the live workshops in the U.S. and abroad, and the online version, it has taken us all over the world to amazing places with phenomenal people. Almost every time I teach anywhere, someone comes up to me to tell me about the magical changes that have happened to them as a result of this work. They are surprised at how easily the changes showed up—quite often they don't even realize that their income has doubled or tripled until they do their taxes, or their year-end summary because it doesn't feel like they are doing anything differently. Things are just working somehow. Money is just coming in. Clients or sales are just showing up.

I know this from direct experience as well. When I was designing and writing the workshop, I tried out all the exercises on myself to make sure they wouldn't result in any unpleasant side effects or spontaneous combustion. I very quickly discovered that I had some beliefs and patterns around money that were, at best, not useful. From those realizations and changes, whole new worlds opened up. When I went to teach the workshop the second time, it occurred to me that it seemed like I had been making more money. So, I checked and discovered that my income since the first workshop had gone up 67% *consistently*—even though I hadn't done anything differently. It was like magic.

Since then life just keeps getting better and more magical—for our participants and me.

I have seen over and over again, how when people are freed from their blocks and patterning around money, they start to flourish. They start to dream. They start to create their lives to be more and more magical, and more and more meaningful.

They start to live.

So, let's try an experiment. This is an old NLP technique (I don't know who created it originally). It's based on the Ghost of Christmas Future from Charles Dickens' *A Christmas Carol*.

Notice where you are in your life right now. Notice what your patterns around money are and have been. Now, imagine going through the rest of your life, all the way to the end of your life, with those patterns. Notice what it's like to have lived your whole life with those patterns. What did you do, or not do? Who was there, or not there? What spaces or things surrounded you? What's it like to have lived that way? And what's it like to leave that life?

Then come back to present time. Now, imagine you were able to change those patterns to *have a much more satisfying experience of life and money*. Imagine going through the rest of your life this way. What do you do, or not do? Who is there or not there? What spaces or things surround you? What's it like to live that way? And what's it like to leave that life?

Now, come back again to present time and compare those two possible futures.

Which one is more the life that you want? Which one is more the life you came here to create? If it's the first one—the track you are currently on, then you don't need to read any further. If, however, the second one has more of what you want—more satisfaction, more freedom, more experiences, more joy—then stay tuned.

I have some options for you.

This is your call.

* NLP (Neuro-Linguistic Programming) comes from the condensed genius of many of the world's best therapists, teachers, entrepreneurs, and motivators. NLP is not based on any theory, but rather on methods and techniques that have consistently produced results.

In short, **NLP is** a compilation of **what works** to get changes for people.

These changes are remarkable not only because of the depth and permanence of the change but also because of the speed and ease with which the change can occur.

CHAPTER TWO

How Your Three Brains Make or Cost You Money

-OR-

Why You Don't Already Have What You Want

---

*"Yesterday I was clever, so I wanted to change the world.
Today I am wise, so I am changing myself."*
—Rumi

At one of our workshops, we met a gifted coach who was wanting to work with women on food, nutrition, and body issues. She had been struggling to start her practice for years, although she had done everything her coaches and the experts told her. Yet in all the years she had been trying to start her practice, the most money she had ever made in a month was $500. The first month after Money Magic, she made $6000—and her income stayed up at that level from then on. Before we talk about how to change your reality, it's important to understand how it is that her reality *hadn't* changed for her previously. She was intelligent, talented, dedicated, and willing to do whatever it took. Still, nothing had changed. What had kept her so stuck? What had kept her stuck is what keeps most people from having what they want.

How Things Get Stuck

(Although the following may sound science-y, it's more of a metaphor and summation to help people understand a little of how they create their experience. The mere fact that I refer to it as "science-y," gives you an idea that I am not attached to hard science or even the strict rules of grammar. I benefit from science every day and have great respect for it, but this is not a scientific paper. I will say, however, that the "metaphors" and summations we have been using for the last 20 years have been increasingly showing up in scientific journals and studies recently as groundbreaking new information.)

NLP is often described as being an operator's manual for the brain. Talking about the brain, however, makes it sound like this monolithic, centralized entity. The brain is actually comprised of several different operating systems patched together with spotty interfacing. In other words, one part of the brain often knoweth not what the other parts are doing.

When most people think of their brain, they think of their cerebral cortex—the big wrinkly lobes on top (this is a context where the more wrinkles you have, the better). The cerebral cortex is in charge of many of the things human beings are most proud of: abstract thought, creativity, meaning, time, (we are the only creatures that seem to experience linear time—this is why you will never see a chicken with a day planner), and perhaps most importantly, understanding consequences.

The cerebral cortex is not fully developed until somewhere between 20-25 years old in women, and 25-30 years old in men. (Or, as my friend Carl says, "Somewhere between 30 and death.") We had been teaching this for years when my partner and I went on a Jeep tour in Sedona, Arizona. We were the only ones on the tour, so we had the guide to ourselves who started telling us stories. In his spare time, he volunteers with the local rescue squad. He said that 90% of the rescues they do involve men 30 and under (who are sure their vehicle can cross whatever terrain they are faced with). He also said that 90% of the snake bites they treat are men 30 and under, and of those snake bites, 95% are bites to the hands or face—not the feet or ankles—which gives you a pretty good idea of what was going on right before the snake had had enough.

He said the responders like to tell this joke:

"What are the first words of English that a snake learns?"

Answer: "Dude, hold my beer!"

This probably is why they don't try to recruit men into the military after 25. A 25-30-year old's brain can compute consequences far better than an 18-year-old's brain, and older men are less likely to volunteer to go places where people get blown up. This also probably explains why you have to be 25 years old in most places to rent a car. (I often hear parents trying to explain consequences to a two or three-year-old whose brain is not capable of making those computations.)

In addition to the cortex, there is the limbic system, which is in charge of emotion. This comes online somewhere between gestation and birth.

Finally, the oldest part of the brain—that some people call the reptile brain—is fully functional in utero. This ancient neurology is shared with every creature on the planet. Its primary objective is survival. It is not concerned with *quality* of life—only with the *quantity* of life. The reptile brain does not care if you are happy. It only cares that you are alive. Not dead=good. Not happy=? (file not found, i.e., irrelevant).

An old joke among biologists is that the creature brain is in charge of the 4 F's: fight, flight, feeding, and reproduction.

What keeps you stuck or struggling with money is mostly held in your creature neurology.

(To be fair, our creature neurology is also what keeps us alive, and if we are not alive none of this really matters.)

Here's how it works in simplified terms: Sometime after conception, the forming organism starts having experiences and making simple associations. There is no thought process yet, but there is sensation/experience, and so the organism starts making simple associations. The first associations often are, "I'm here, and it's like this." The organism assumes a correlation. So, if a child comes into a family and there is stress or tension, the forming neurology will associate the two. "I'm here, and it's tense and scary. It must be me," or "life must be scary and dangerous," or both. Not all associations are bad, and so we end up with a mixture of varied and sometimes contradictory associations, such as, "The world is dangerous." "The world is safe and loving. I am loved." "I am the cause of stress and unhappiness," etc. These associations are learnings the child is making about the world, themselves, and life. These learnings become automated. It's incredibly useful that learnings become automated, because otherwise when you woke up each morning, you would have to relearn how to walk, talk, control your bladder, and everything else you've ever learned. Unfortunately, however, some of the learnings that become automated are along the lines of: "The world isn't safe." "There's not enough." "It's selfish to want things." "Money is stressful." "Money is hard to get." "You have to sacrifice and struggle to have money." Or, "I'm not enough." Once those learnings become automated, they are like reflexes. If later in life we learn different possibilities such as: "Life can be good." "You can make money doing what you love." "There is enough for everyone," etc. these later learnings do not replace the earlier associations, because the later learnings are stored in different areas of the brain. *To actually change the automated learnings, you have to access the parts of the brain that were developing when the original learnings/associations occurred.*

*This is what the change patterns of Money Magic do. And it's why the changes are so easy, and permanent—because it is like rewriting software. If you know how to rewrite software, and you know the code it's written in, you can rewrite the code and then the program runs differently, and **automatically**. You don't have to encourage the software ("Go little software!"); you don't have to do affirmations ("You are powerful software"); you don't have to hold the software accountable. ("We agreed that you would run the new code now.") The software runs the new programming automatically.*

This is also why willpower doesn't work.

Why Willpower Doesn't Work

Willpower is a way we try to force ourselves to overcome our natural tendencies—our automatic patterning. We try harder to be different. We try to wrestle ourselves to the ground, hold our own feet to the fire, and force ourselves to do or be different.

Willpower is a lot of work.

Willpower is a fight with ourselves. As my friend Carl Buchheit says, "When you fight with yourself, who actually wins?"

Willpower rarely produces significant, lasting change.

By the time most of us are adults, the blocks that are in our way are not conscious. **If they were conscious, we would have changed them already**. Nobody consciously creates the experience of problems, blocks or limitations around money. The blocks and limitations are subconscious patterning. They are reflexive. They are part of our mental software. Trying to consciously override our subconscious patterning is a little like yelling at your computer and expecting it to respond differently (which I have tried many times, by the way, so I know it doesn't work). It's like trying not to move your leg when the doctor hits your knee in the reflex spot. It's like trying to get your pupils not to constrict when someone shines a bright light in your eyes. The patterning is reflexive.

If you have patterning to struggle around money, and you force yourself to create more money, the pattern will assert itself somehow. When people use willpower to force themselves to make more money, they often end up with unexpected losses or bills that somehow eat up all the extra earnings, and they end up right back where they started, or in an even worse place. If a plane is on autopilot to maintain a certain altitude, it will automatically act to correct or compensate for any dips or lifts. Many people are on financial autopilot to maintain a certain level of income/struggle/limitation. No matter what they do to change it, their subconscious patterning corrects for it—often in confounding and mysterious ways.

(When patterning revises, however, the opposite seems to happen. People tell me all the time after taking my class that they are making more money (often tripling their income) but that they don't feel like they are doing anything differently. I hear that sentence over and over from graduates.

There's no willpower involved. There's no need for it. Because their autopilot is now set to maintain a different financial altitude (and the change seems to just happen—often in mysterious and wonderful ways.)

When Your Money Patterning Is Created

Most of your patterning—by which I mean, most of your subconscious beliefs (associations), are in place between the ages of three to six years old. In fact, the brain undergoes a huge pruning around the age of three, where it gets rid of two-thirds of its neurons. The ones it keeps are the ones most being used. So, if there has been a lot of stress or struggle, those are the bulk of the neurons and neural pathways that will be kept. (There is still an almost infinite amount of recombinations possible from the neurons that are kept—and this is where the change patterns come into play later.)

The effect of this is that most of the fundamental patterns, beliefs and associations that we have about ourselves, life, and money are in place before we have developed any real executive function—that is to say, before we are truly old enough to think for ourselves and see life and possibility from a broader perspective. When, later in life, our perspective of who we are, and what we want, and what is possible for us, expands, it does not change the original patterning. It just gets layered on top of the foundational patterning, and is often diminished, or flat-out counteracted by the original patterning.

One of our participants came from a very difficult and dangerous upbringing. When she took our workshop, she was a single mother and life was challenging. She had been struggling most of her life and had only about $700 in the bank. A lot of the change patterns she did focused on accessing and updating those old internal software programs she was running so that her neurology--especially her creature neurology--could know that it was safer now, that she had made it, and that life and money could be much easier. In the two weeks after the workshop, she had made over $25,000. People just kept finding her and calling her and asking her how they could work with her and pay her. She didn't go out and find these people. *They found her. They asked her if they could pay her.* Because when the subconscious, automatic patterning changed for her, her life and her reality shifted to match the new patterning. Some of these changes are neurological (more on that later, too), and some are downright inexplicable. It is the quantum effect—the law of attraction—the mirroring universe. Call it what you will, but we have seen it happen over and over again for participants. And it feels like magic.

If you don't have what you want, it's not because you are broken, lazy, or stupid.

It's because you have something in the way.

Nothing more.

And now that we know patterning can be changed; a very important question becomes relevant.

It's a simple question, but the longer I do this, the more I realize how profound it is.

It is a life-changing question.

It is the Alpha and the omega, and then, the Alpha again.

So, when *you are ready,* we have a question for you.

CHAPTER THREE

The Life-Changing Question
-OR-
Your Compass for Life and Money

---

*"If one does not know to which port one is sailing,
no wind is favorable."*
—Seneca

Thirty or more years ago, I was Christmas shopping and found a book I really liked titled, *The Book of Questions*, and so I bought it and gave it as a gift to someone. A few months later, I asked her if she liked the book. She said, "I never got past the first page." I looked at the first page to see what had stopped her in her tracks, and on it was the single question, "What would you attempt if you knew you could not fail?"

It is a mind-expanding question that requires you to set aside all your fears and doubts and to simply dream. It is another way of asking one of life's most important questions, which is "What would you like?"

So, what would you like?

Even if you don't think it's possible, ask yourself what would you like in your life, and in your money?

The question "What would you like?" is a simple but very profound one. It asks you to be in the driver's seat of your life and make choices about where you want to go, what you want to experience, and how you want to engage with life.

It is through our wants and desires that we reach out to life.

And when we reach out to life, life expands. Consciousness expands. We enjoy a better quality of life because generations before us wanted something better.

Desire is attractive. It pulls what we want to us, in magical ways.

Years ago, after having been invited to teach in Australia a couple of years in a row, we decided to go back on our own to teach, without having been invited by anyone—which meant doing all the promotion ourselves (not my strong suit). I calculated how much it would cost for the two of us to go there for two weeks, rent out workshop space, and then tallied up lost income, etc., and it came to about $25,000 to break even. That was a lot of money at the time, and I started to panic a little.

Then I remembered what I do.

So, I asked myself how much I wanted to make in **profit** and came up with a number that felt good. I felt clear. Then, *I forgot about it.* That was all. I didn't create an action plan; I didn't figure out how many participants we would need-nothing, nada, rien. I did a webinar we had planned and sent out some emails. That was it.

When we got home, and I added up all the expenses and income; we were $106 dollars over the profit I had decided on.

A participant who took our online class was making the amount of money he wanted, but he wanted to see his kids and have time with his family. He said he couldn't work less, because they needed that amount of income, but he did want more time with his family. Within two weeks of starting the class, he was picking his kids up from school every day, having time with them, being home for dinner every night AND he was still making the same amount of money. He couldn't figure out how it was happening, which freaked him out a little, but it was happening.

Desire is a powerful thing. And when you clear up the patterning that's in the way, things show up quickly and powerfully. When the patterning that was in his way changed, suddenly he was making the same amount of money and working fewer hours.

Another woman who took the online class wasn't working, (and didn't really want to) but she did want some things for her family, such as, a car, a vacation, and a few other things. By the end of the class, out of the blue, different people had come out of the woodwork and given her everything on her list.

For some people the question "What do I want?" is not something they feel okay asking themselves. It feels selfish, and they have been taught that is wrong.

> *Selfishness is defined by the Merriam-Webster dictionary as "Having or showing concern only for yourself and not for the needs or feelings of other people: concerned excessively or exclusively with oneself: seeking or concentrating on one's own advantage, pleasure, or well-being without regard for others"*
>
> **It is not the wanting that makes something selfish—it is the complete disregard for others.**

Wanting something for yourself does not mean you don't care for others.

Human beings are the only species on our planet that make themselves crazy over this. I don't pretend to know what goes on in the mind of the average golden retriever, but I am pretty sure this conversation has never happened in one of their heads:

"My human is offering me a cookie. Is okay for me to have a cookie? Have I had too many cookies? Do all the other dogs in the world have cookies? Will my person think less of me for wanting the cookie? Am I a bad dog to want the cookie?"

(Sadly, this is pretty close to what happens in *my* head when someone offers me a cookie, but the average golden retriever—arguably one of the most loving creatures on the planet, is not troubled by this kind of self-doubt and recrimination.)

A golden retriever is clear it wants the cookie. And love and attention. And toys and play. In fact, if it didn't want those things, then something might be wrong.

Our front yard has a redwood tree that is well over a hundred years old. It does not seem to be questioning whether it is okay to reach for the sun and take the water and nutrients it seeks. It is designed to grow and reach. And so are we.

As humans, we are designed to both care for others and want things for ourselves. People who don't want anything are often not very engaged in life.

So, let's let you engage a little bit, even if it's only in your imagination, and get clearer on what you want. Desire plus clarity is even more powerful than desire alone. (And there is some very sophisticated physics indicating that when you think a thought, not only does that thought exist, that thought actually begins thinking—

MONEY MAGIC

your thoughts don't just happen in the privacy of your head. They are creations in and of themselves--creations that begin thinking, which creates more creations that begin thinking. Every positive, happy thought you think begins creating worlds of their own.)

At the end of this chapter, you can take yourself through a popular change piece from the Money Magic workshop where you can start laying down neurological pathways to what you want. But first, it helps to get clear about what that is.

So, with that in mind, it's time to get started. It's all about choice.

It all begins with you reaching out to life.

It all begins with what you want...

(The following questions are from NLP Marin's version of something called The Outcome Frame)

What would you like (regarding money)?

When you have that, what will having that do for you? (I.e., what good thing comes from having that?)

Where, when and with whom do you want it?

How will you know that you have it? (What will be happening in your life, how will you feel on the inside, physically and emotionally, etc.?)

How will having this affect other important aspects of your life, such as family, partner, etc.? (Another way to ask this is, is there anything that you might lose that you value? If there is, see if you can imagine having what you want without having to lose that which you value.)

When you are clear on what you want, take a moment to imagine yourself having that, and see yourself from the outside--as though you were someone else watching you from across the street. Notice how that will be. Then imagine stepping into the version of you that has what you want and notice what it's like to be inside that you. Look through your eyes; breathe with your lungs and notice what you say to yourself when *you have that experience*. Take a few moments to **let that sink in.**

Then, if **you are ready to move toward that,** you can **now** do this change pattern:

Change Piece: Emerging Experience

(This is an adaptation of Robert Dilts' Belief Chain with a specialized script that I wrote for Money Magic. It teaches your brain a sequence on how to get from where you are to where you want to be by creating neurological associations that become automatic. If you are listening to this in an audiobook, don't do this, or any of the change patterns, while driving, operating heavy machinery, or doing anything that could be dangerous, or embarrassing, if you were to get sleepy or trancey.)

Get five pieces of paper.

On one of them, write what you want (based on the questions above).

On the second piece of paper, write what your current situation is. For example, if what you want is to be making $200,000 a year with a balanced lifestyle, and what you are currently experiencing is working way too hard for $30,000 a year, then one piece of paper would say, "$200,000 a year with a balanced lifestyle," and the other would say, "$30,000 a year working too hard."

On the remaining three pieces of paper, put a +1 on one, a +2 on another, and a +3 on the third.

Then lay them out in a line, about a step apart each, with your current experience first, then +1, +2, +3 and ending with what you want. It should look like this:

You will start with your current experience and proceed through each step according to the following instructions. (The first time through will be slow. Allow yourself to imagine each step as vividly as you can. **What matters most is how it feels.** After the first time through, however, you will just be walking through the sequence without having to spend a lot of time imagining.)

Current Experience

So, as you step onto the first marker, notice your current situation in the area that is about to change. It's probably very familiar. In fact, it's old news, but at one point it was an important step, so take a minute to appreciate it for the part of your progression that it was. As you recall how it has been up until now, notice how things looked and sounded and felt when this was what was happening. Notice how your body felt, what your posture and breathing were, and how your inner dialogue sounded. Notice the conditions of your life that seemed to go with it. And notice what you were believing and who you were being in the midst of all that. This is the experience that is on its way out. In fact, it has already reached completion, or you wouldn't be motivated to *make this change.* So, appreciate it for what it was, and know that **you will be okay.** In fact, that completion and that okayness is pulling the next step towards you, even as you move towards it, just as when you finish letting a breath out, there is an instinctive pull to bring the next breath in, isn't there?

So, when **you are ready**,

Step onto the next marker.

+1

As you step onto this spot, notice the first thing that has begun to shift on the way to the experience you want. Notice how things look, and sound, and feel, when things are mostly the way they've been, but there are beginning to be signs of what you want showing up. Notice how your body feels, what your posture and breathing are like when **you are starting to have elements appear of what you want.**

What is the inner dialogue that goes with this?

Notice the conditions of your life that reflect that **what you want is beginning to show up.**

And, finally, notice what you are believing and who you are being when **the first signs of what you want are there now.**

As that begins to become familiar you may become aware that **the next step is already pulling you forward.** Just as when one foot makes solid contact with the ground, the other foot is **already moving ahead,**

And so, as **you are ready**, step onto the next marker.

+2

As you step onto this spot, notice what it is like when you are experiencing some of how it used to be and some of what you want now, in almost equal measure, halfway between what was and what is becoming the way it is now. Both present, both possible, both available.

Notice how things look and sound and feel when you are experiencing elements of both how it had been, and how it is becoming.

Notice what you say to yourself as you notice **this phase is already passing,** and the next step is already moving toward you, as you step forward into it.

+3

As you step onto this spot, notice what it's like when the new experience that has been emerging, is now your predominant experience, and the way that it had been up until recently is fading into completion. Notice how there are only vestiges and remnants of how things were, passing as all things do, and leaving increasing space and attention to notice what it is like when **what is mostly present is your emerging desired experience.** Notice how things look and sound and feel when **you are experiencing so much of what you want.**

Notice what you say to yourself as **it becomes time for that emerging reality to be fully present now,** moving you onto the next marker, and into the full realization of what you want.

What You Want

Now that **you have stepped fully into what you want,** take a moment to appreciate fully the experience of this. Notice how things look here. Notice how things sound. Notice how things feel, emotionally, energetically, and in your body. Notice your posture and breathing. Notice even how things smell and taste in this new chosen reality. Notice that as the way things used to be was a stepping stone to this place, this place will eventually be a stepping stone to something even fuller, but for now, allow yourself the grace of **having what you have created now.** Breathe into your belly and allow this to soak into the fabric of your being.

When you have had ample to time to appreciate and marinate in that experience, step off the marker and walk around a bit.

Then walk through the sequence again and again, but going much faster each time, so that you are practically skipping toward the end, but always spend the most time on the last spot (the What You Want spot,) and always walk around randomly before you start again. Don't ever go directly from What You Want back to the Current Experience. We want to teach your brain a sequence-not a loop.

Go through the sequence quickly at least 15 times (the last 10 times are like speed walking or skipping to the What You Want spot).

Then go do something fun, and let your brain integrate a little.

CHAPTER FOUR

The Glasses You Don't Know You are Wearing
-OR-
How to Spot Your Core Beliefs

"We don't see things as they are. We see them as we are."
—Talmud

Once Upon a Time in Circuit City

Some years back, a friend of mine wanted to buy a CD player (it was that long ago). There are few pleasures that compare with buying electronics for me, so I very cheerfully offered to help her. I suggested we go to Circuit City (this chain of stores closed a while back, but at the time they had a wide selection of all things technologically inclined.) I had been to Circuit City many times and had always had good experiences there. The salespeople were friendly and helpful, and I always found what I wanted at a good price. So, I was surprised when my friend said to me, "Oh no, not there. Their service is terrible." But I assured her that it would be good--that I went there all the time and we could find her a good CD player. She reluctantly agreed and off we went. We entered the store, and for the first time in my experience, there was not a soul in sight. It was like one of those scenes in a ghost town in an Old Western; it was deserted and silent. I half expected to see tumble-weeds blowing down the aisles. It took us 10 minutes to find anyone who worked there, and when we did, they were surly and unhelpful. So, we left. I couldn't believe it. This had never happened before. A month or so later, I wanted to buy something else electronic and thought about going to Circuit City, and then almost changed my mind because of the last experience with my friend. But I decided to go back once more and give it a try. I walked in and was immediately greeted by several cheerful salespeople, one of whom helped me find just what I needed, and within 10 minutes my new electronic friend and I were on our way home. The difference was so striking. Every time my friend went to Circuit City she had a bad experience. Every time I went, except when I went with her, I had a good experience.

So, which one of us was right? Which was the real Circuit City? And the answer was both. She got her version of reality, and I got mine. Circuit City was a screen we were both projecting our reality (beliefs) on.

We all do this with everything in our lives all the time.

It seems to us as though there is a solid, objective reality that we all experience, but, in fact, what's "out there" is screen after screen after screen upon which we continually project our subconscious, automated beliefs.

There's an old Zen story which sums this up perfectly.

A monk was out tending his vines near a path that led from the mountain village, down to the valley village. One morning, a traveler came whistling down the path and saw the monk. "Excuse me," he

MONEY MAGIC

said. "I'm heading down to the valley village. Do you know what it's like there?"

"Have you just come from the mountain village?" the monk asked. When the traveler confirmed that he had just come from there; the monk asked, "What was it like up there in the mountain village?"

The traveler replied, "It was wonderful. The people were warm and friendly. The children were full of life and curiosity. It was just great."

The monk said, "I think you will find it's pretty much the same down in the valley." Satisfied, the traveler went happily on his way.

A little while later, another traveler came trudging down the same path. He, too, saw the monk and asked him what the valley village was like.

The monk asked him, "Have you just come from the mountain village?"

"Unfortunately, yes," answered the second traveler.

"What was it like there?" asked the monk.

"It was just awful," said the traveler. "The people were rude and unfriendly. The children were wild and unruly. I couldn't leave fast enough."

The monk looked at him and said, "I think you will find it's pretty much the same down in the valley."

If you swap out one of those villages for an electronics store, you pretty much have my experience with my friend at Circuit City.

The quote at the beginning of this chapter from the Talmud was in reference to dream interpretation, but it applies to the waking dream we call life as well.

R.C. Peck, the founder of Fearless Wealth (and also the person who has helped me the most with my investments), says, "We move at the speed of our beliefs."

This is not just new age, woo woo, hippy philosophy. (By the way, I do not mean to disparage new age, woo woo, hippy philosophy-it's pretty much what I live for, but if this has all been a little hard to swallow, here's some science for you.) There is something in human brains called The Reticular Activating System. The RAS is a function of your brain that is **designed to look for what it is already looking for and to filter out what it is not looking for.**

The most common experience people often have of noticing this is when they are thinking about buying a new car. Let's say you have been thinking of buying a new car, and you decide on a certain type, or model, for example, a red Jeep. Somehow, overnight, the roads and parking lots of your city or town, fill up with that kind of car. Suddenly red Jeeps are everywhere. Because once your attention, conscious or subconscious, is focused on jeeps, the RAS filters your perception to see Jeeps.

The RAS also deletes what it is not looking for.

Pregnant women (and women who want to be pregnant) tell me that the world is filled with pregnant women. I almost never see them. My RAS is not sorting for them.

In the documentary film *What the Bleep Do We Know?* a woman told a story about when the Spanish first came to the New World. She said that the natives, at first, couldn't see the ships because their brains had no reference for clipper ships. So, what they saw were men floating in the air above the water, and they thought, *these must be gods.* The shaman, who was used to seeing beyond what was known, eventually saw the ships and told the rest about them. Soon all of them could see the ships. There's no way to know if this story is true, or apocryphal, but it is an accurate description of how our brains filter and distort what we call reality.

Our old patterning, i.e., our subconscious beliefs and associations, are largely what determine what our brains filter in, and what they filter out.

And because our RAS filters in what matches our beliefs, and filters out what doesn't, we continually experience things that match our subconscious filters and delete everything that doesn't match them.

How to Spot Your Core Beliefs

We often hear ourselves and others state what we believe.

"I believe that all people should have basic human rights."

"I believe that a free market system benefits everyone."

"I believe that God will punish wrongdoers."

These are examples of things people consciously assert as beliefs. These may be dearly held criteria, but they are not necessarily core beliefs. In fact, if you can state or recognize something as a belief, it probably is not a core belief. This is because **our core beliefs are invisible** to us as beliefs. *Our core beliefs are just the way life is.* Anytime you or someone else says, "that's not a belief; that's just the way it is," you are hearing a core belief.

Here's the secret to spotting a core belief in your life:

Look at the things that happen in your life—the kind of relationships you have, your experience of work, money, life, health—these are the out-picturing of your core beliefs.

The things that happen to you that seem to be outside of your control are the manifestations of your core beliefs.

In fact, everything that you, or anyone, asserts about how things are, how life works, or what is true, is an assertion of a core belief. **The more certain you are that you are right about something, the more certain it is that you are expressing a core belief.**

To spot your core beliefs around money, notice what you have experienced around money in your life.

Has there been enough? Have you had to work hard to get it? Do you have to suffer or do things you don't want to do to get it? Do people take it away from you? Do you lose it? If you start to make money, do you spend it all? Are people untrustworthy around it? Do you not seem to have control around how much you make or have or keep? Can you count on it being there for you? Is life hard or unpredictable?

To get a sense of some of your core beliefs around money, you can fill in the following statements. (I don't know where these came from originally. I first saw them when I was teaching with Peggy O'Neal, a professional business coach in the mid-1990s. John Overdorf, a psychologist, and wonderful NLP Trainer, told me they were floating around in psychiatric circles back in the 1980's.)

Write down the first thing that pops into your head—not necessarily what you want the answer to be, but your very first response. The faster you do this, the better, so that you don't give yourself a chance to think about it. Just let yourself respond.

Complete the following phrases (without editing in your head):

1. People with money are _____.

2. Money makes people _____.

3. I'd have more money if _____.

4. My father thought money was _____.

5. My mother thought money was _____.

6. I'd be more successful if _____.

7. In my family, money _____.

8. Money equals _____.

9. If I were successful, I'd _____.

10. If I could afford it, I'd _____.

11. I'm afraid that if I had money I'd _____.

12. Money is _____.

13. Money causes _____.

14. In order to be more successful, I'd need to _____.

15. When I feel successful, I usually _____.

16. When I see other people being successful, I usually _____.

17. Having money is not _____.

18. In order to have more money, I'd need to _____.

MICHELLE MASTERS

19. When I have money,
    I usually _____.

20. I think money _____.

21. My father could never _____.

22. My mother could never _____.

23. People think money _____.

24. A person can be successful if _____.

25. Being broke tells me _____.

26. Looking through my father's eyes,
    I am _____.

27. Looking through my mother's eyes,
    I am _____.

28. If I did better than my father financially,
    then _____.

29. If I did better than my mother financially,
    then _____.

30. Success always _____.

31. I deserve _____.

32. I don't deserve _____.

33. People deserve to have money if _____.

If some of your answers surprised you or describe a life or circumstances that you don't want, then changing those subconscious responses and beliefs can make a huge difference in your life. **Whether you consciously believe the words or phrases that popped up, or** not, those associations are there in your head, which means they are part of what your subconscious filters. It means they are a part of your money world.

Common Limiting Beliefs About Money

Here are some of the most common beliefs I find when I'm working with people on their money patterns:

- You have to work hard to make money
- You have to work hard to deserve money
- The harder you work, the more deserving you are
- You (I) are/am not doing enough
- You (I) are/am not enough
- There is not enough
- There is not enough for everyone
- Money causes strife/problems
- Wanting money is shallow/materialistic/wrong/selfish
- Spiritual/good people are not interested in money
- Wanting money/good things for yourself means that you are selfish and don't care about other people
- It is more caring to give money away
- People will be jealous if you have money
- It's not okay to have money when others don't
- You (I) don't deserve to have money

Without a way to change these kinds of beliefs, they act like giant boulders we are chained to—keeping us from moving very far or very fast.

But now we have a way to change these patterns and update the old software that you have running.

The most amazing part of this all is that **when you change a core belief, your life fundamentally changes**—often in ways you could never have imagined. When a core belief changes, the world seems to change. We actually begin to have a different experience of life without trying to be different—it's just different.

> *A workshop participant saw me the weekend after taking the class and told me that in the three days since the class $25,000 worth of business had come to him. He said, "Usually I have to go looking for business, but this came knocking on my door looking for me. I didn't have to do anything."*
>
> *Another participant came back to take the class again because he told me that about a month after he had taken it for the first time he suddenly started getting calls out of the blue for really big contracts. It was so noticeably different that he found himself asking himself, why am I getting all these big contracts now? and then he remembered what he had worked on in the class. It ended up being his best year ever. When he came back to take the class again he was already surpassing that best year ever, and he was only a few months into the year—and* **he wasn't doing anything different consciously.** *This is where it feels like magic.*

When core beliefs change, lives change. Circumstances change. Even people seem to change. It happens over and over again.

So, with that in mind, here is an opportunity to change one, or more, of your old patterns.

Change Pattern: Revising A Past Belief

(This is an adaptation of another brilliant Robert Dilts' change pattern, combined with something called a Trans-Derivational Search. This is a specific script that I wrote for Money Magic, using some of Robert Dilts' structure. It allows you to access the origin of a limiting belief/association, and to update the old meanings that were made, and to create new, automatic neural associations.)

For this change pattern, you will need two spatial markers. These can be two pieces of paper that you place on the floor when instructed to mark a certain location.

1. Find a place where you can allow yourself to walk backward at least 6-10 feet (2-3 meters). With that amount of space behind you, place one of your markers between your feet. This represents Now. Look directly behind you. Imagine your entire past lies behind you (within that 6-10 feet) and choose a spot to represent the beginning of your life.

2. Think about the belief/association around money that you want to change. Notice how it feels.

3. Then, without thinking about, but noticing the feeling of the belief, allow your body to move backward through time until you come to the place where the feeling began. Just let your body stop on its own.

4. When your body stops, notice what it feels like here. How old do you feel? Where does it feel like you are? Who is there, or not there? What was happening then? And what did you decide this meant—about you, or life, or money? When you have noticed everything that seemed to be important about that experience, place the second marker between your feet and then step out of that spot.

47

5. Now, imagine that the spot you just stepped out of, is in the center of a large grid like this one on the floor.

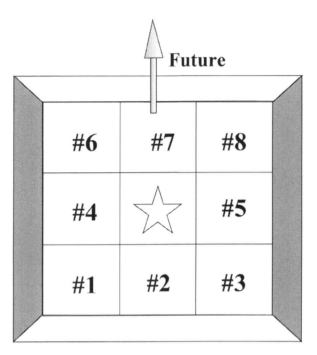

6. Now imagine that standing in Spot #1 (behind you to your left) is someone who you know (from any time in your life) who cares for you, and who you trust, with a perspective on this that could be useful for you. When you can see them there, step into that person in Spot #1 and notice their encouragement and perspective for the younger you. When you can feel that, take all of that feeling and awareness and step back into the center spot and breathe that through the younger you—imagining you are in the body of the younger you. Breathe into your belly and *allow that to settle in*.

MONEY MAGIC

7. Then look directly behind you at Spot #2. Imagine there a mythical or fictional hero of yours. Remember a character who used to be, or still is, a hero of yours, who has qualities you admire. See them there. Then step into the energy of that hero and notice what awareness or abilities they have to offer that younger you. When you can feel that, take all of that feeling and awareness and step back into the center, breathing that into and through the younger you.

8. Then look behind you to your right at Spot #3. Imagine there a supportive ancestor. Possibly someone unknown from long ago. Someone who wants to see you and the family do well. Step into them and feel their support and blessing for that younger you. When you can feel that, take all of that feeling and awareness and blessing and step back into the center spot, into the body of the younger you, and breathe that through your body, noticing that *you have support now.*

9. Then, look directly to your left at Spot #4. Picture there a wise counselor. Someone real or archetypal who has a profound understanding or perspective for that younger you. Step into them and notice their wisdom about this. When you can feel that, take all of that feeling and awareness and step back into the center spot and breathe that through the younger you, noticing how already *that wisdom is starting to spread throughout your body, your past, and your future now.*

10. Then look directly to your right at Spot #5. Imagine there a role model. Someone in the world who has skills or abilities that would be beneficial for the younger you, as a role model. When you can see them there, step into them and notice the most useful parts of them and their abili-

ties. When you can feel those useful abilities, take all of that and, step back into the center spot and breathe that through the younger you, noticing what it's like when *you have those abilities now*.

11. Then look in front of you to Spot #6. Imagine standing there, someone you adore. See a person (or animal) that you absolutely adore in front of you to the left in Spot #6. See them there and feel your adoration for them. Then step into them and notice that feeling of being adored. When you can feel that, take that feeling of being adored and step back into the center, and breathe that through the younger you. This is just a tiny fraction of how much *the universe adores you*.

12. Then look directly in front of you at Spot #7. Imagine there a slightly future version of you who has overcome the obstacles the younger you was dealing with. Step into that you and notice what encouragement, advice, and/or resources they have to share with the younger you. When you can feel that, take all of that feeling and awareness and, step back into the center spot and breathe that through the younger you.

13. Then look in front of you to your right at Spot #8. Imagine there a satisfied you at the end of your life. A you who has had a full, rich experience of life. Step into that future you and notice the satisfaction and fulfillment of a life lived and lived well. Notice what gifts of wisdom, gratitude and appreciation they have for the younger you. When you can feel that, take all of that feeling and awareness and step back into the center spot and breathe that through the younger you, breathing into your belly.

Allow that and all the combined support, wisdom, encouragement and resources from all these sources to integrate throughout the body, heart, and mind of the younger you. Take a moment to notice all of them around you.

Behind you, is the person who cares for you, the fictional hero, and a supportive ancestor.

Next to you, on one side is the wise counselor, and on the other side the role model.

In front of you, is the one you adore, and the future versions of you, all of whom are rooting for you.

Then out in your future, notice the future you imagined in the previous change pattern—a more fulfilling experience of life and money, there, already waiting for you.

Take a moment to notice all the other places in time where **decisions related to money** are available to **revise and update now** and **allow those to reorganize usefully, in time, and outside of time, NOW. As that is completing,**

And seeing that **all of these sources of support are there with you now,** and when you are ready, begin to move forward toward your future, allowing all of these perspectives, gifts, and resources to integrate throughout time as **you grow increasingly into them,** and as the future gets closer and more solidly available with each step.

With each step notice that all of these sources of **support** walk **with you.** Move forward at your own pace until all of that becomes integrated and present in current time, **now.**

Stop when you reach the marker for Now.

CHAPTER FIVE

The Invisible Ceiling
-OR-
Money, Worth and Deserving

"We are made of star stuff."
—Carl Sagan

Two weeks after one of my workshops, a participant contacted me because of something that had happened, which had him in a panic. He told me that he had thought he didn't need the workshop because his company was worth $20 million, but it was part of a larger program that he was taking, so he came. One of the exercises in the workshop was particularly impactful for him, and something profound fundamentally shifted inside him.

Then, out of the blue, in the first few days after the workshop, he got an unexpected offer. The offer would take his company from a $20 million-venture to over a billion dollars. He wasn't expecting that or prepared for it, and he found himself having suicidal thoughts and behaviors.

He thought he was fine with money, but he had an invisible ceiling—a limit on how much he would let himself have--and the offer was way beyond the limit. Until this happened, he didn't even know he had a limit.

We all have an invisible ceiling. Some of us have high ceilings, and some of us have very low ceilings, but we all have a limit on how much we will let ourselves have. And if we somehow exceed our limit, we typically find a way to get rid of the extra or destroy something else in our lives to balance out the equation.

There are a couple of things that determine our ceiling, but one of the biggest is our sense of our own worth.

What do you think you are worth?

It's a very loaded question, and later in this chapter I will tell you a very simple way to find out what you actually think you are worth, but it fundamentally determines how good you will let life be for you—how much love, happiness, health, friends, and money you will let yourself have.

When I was in college, I had to direct a one-act play for a class I was taking. The play I chose was called *The Zoo Story*. In part of it, one character asks the other a series of questions, like,

"Where do you live?" "Are you married?" "What do you do?" "How much do you make?"

The teacher of the class called me over at one point and asked about the series of questions. He said, "You have the character asking the question about how much the other one makes the same way he's asking all the other questions." Then he said, "I would rather have someone ask me why my marriage failed than ask me how much I make." That was a revelation for me. It was my first insight into how deeply money is connected to our sense of our own worth. In fact, in the U.S., in order to ask how much money someone makes, one often asks, "How much is he/she worth?"

I was having lunch with someone recently who was surprised and a little dismayed that friends of hers had told her how much money they make. "That's too personal," she said. "I don't need to know that." There is both fear and deep shame attached quite often to how much money we have or make (or how much we don't have or don't make). I never understood why when I asked a bank teller what my balance was, instead of just answering me, they would write it silently on a piece of paper and pass it to me like a wartime secret, but in light of this topic, it makes sense to me now. They think they are protecting my privacy or my sense of pride.

Asking how much you are worth is like asking how much you deserve because we will not let ourselves have, or keep, more than we think we deserve.

Given how fundamental our sense of worth is to everything we experience (or don't experience) in life, it is astounding to realize that **our basic sense of our own worth is in place by 3-4 years old.** The beliefs we develop about ourselves and the world in those first four years become the foundation upon which we build our life and identity. Even if later in life we get a broader sense of our worth, it will still rest on that early foundation.

In classic Jungian dream interpretation, houses often represent our identity. (Both are artificial constructions that we live inside to feel safe.) Moving, or remodeling a house, in a dream can be a symbol for changing or revising your identity. If we use that metaphor of a house representing the identity, with each year we live, it's as though we add another level onto the house, i.e., someone who is 30 would be represented as a 30-floor building. Since our sense of worth is our foundation, if our sense of our own worth is shaky, so is our foundation. How much life, happiness, money and success we can allow depends on how solid our foundation is—and how wide.

One of my dearest friends once bought a house that we all tried to talk her out of. It had burned out furniture in front of it, a flea infestation, arsenic in the well water, appliances that had bare wires stuck into electrical outlets (instead of plugs), a heater that was giving off lethal doses of carbon monoxide gas, and, most troubling for me, a suspicious foundation.

The house was built on a slope, so part of it rested on the hill, and the rest was, in theory, supported by a load-bearing beam that the house could rest on. HOWEVER, between the bottom of the house frame and the top of the load bearing beam was a gap of about 5-6 inches. To bridge that gap, someone had stacked about 20 quarter inch shims into a tiny tower. (A shim is a small, thin piece of wood meant to fill a very small gap—like something you would put under a restaurant table to keep it from wobbling. In this case, the shims were 2-inch squares that were a quarter of an inch thick.) A stack of shims was supporting her house. I should add that this is in California, where the earth regularly moves and quakes. If she were to try to add anything onto the house, it would be in danger of collapsing.

Most of us have some of our identity/sense of worth resting on a solid foundation, and some of it is supported by shims or nothing at all. If you try to add a lot of wealth onto a shaky foundation, the whole structure becomes unstable. Stories of athletes or celebrities who become suddenly successful and then blow up their lives, health, relationships, or careers within a few years, are commonplace in the news. In Britain, "lotto louts" describes people who win the lottery and then spectacularly destroy their lives, because what they won is much bigger than what they actually think they deserve. And so, they get rid of it.

MONEY MAGIC

To try to shim up the gaps in our sense of our own worth, we often barter for it with hard work, struggle and sacrifice. The hard work, struggle and sacrifice seem to justify letting ourselves have good things. I can't tell you how many people I have heard justify the beautiful house or money they have by saying, "Yeah, but I worked hard for it." I remember even hearing President Obama in a speech saying something like, "If you come to this country, and you work hard..." and I thought, *et tu, Barack?*

"But I've already worked on that." I hear from a lot of clients and participants that they have worked to improve their sense of their own worth. Typically, however, they have worked as adults, in therapy or personal growth workshops to expand their sense of worth. This is good, but *remodeling the 30th or 44th floor doesn't change the foundation.* It just gives you a solid floor sitting on a shaky foundation. (To revise the foundation, you have to access the parts of the brain that were developing when the foundations were laid. This is what the change patterns do so well.)

So, here's the secret to discovering what you think you deserve.

If you want to know what you think you are worth, look at what your life is like. What will you let yourself have, and experience, consistently?

And can it be easy and fun?

Let's try an experiment.

Change Pattern: Expanding Your Sense of Worth

Picture for a moment the infinite worth that you came from. Imagine you can go back and watch yourself incarnate from that place. From the outside, watch yourself come into a brand new developing body. As you watch yourself grow and develop, from conception onwards, through childhood all the way to your current age, when does that innate sense of infinite worth begin to diminish? Does it happen right away, or does it diminish over time? Just watch from the outside and notice what happens.

Now take a minute to notice, that however small you may feel...

you are a part of the infinite expression of the universe.

And even a tiny piece of infinity is infinite.

You are star stuff.

*Now, think of a symbol to represent the infinite worth that you came from. Imagine you can go back again and watch yourself incarnate with that symbol of your infinite worth in every cell of your developing body. Then, imagine **stepping into that** developing body, with that symbol of **infinite worth** multiplying through all the developing cells and tissue of your new body. Let yourself **marinate in that experience of worth** until you are ready to be born. Then, leaving all the details of your past and your family aside, notice what it's like to come into the world with the infinite worth of the universe in every cell of your being, permeating your heart, and belly, and both hemispheres of your developing brain. Breathe that experience of worth into your belly. Breathe it into your heart. Breathe it into the left hemisphere of your brain, and then from the left hemisphere into the right hemisphere and back again.*

*When **you are ready,** allow yourself to grow up from that new-born body all the way to your current adult age, saying to yourself all along the way, "I am. And I am here."*

*When that feels complete, notice how this changes your experience of life, yourself, the world and money. **Let** the best parts of **that soak into** the fabric of **your being,** in whatever ways feel most appropriate to you.*

CHAPTER SIX

What's in Your Personals Ad?
-OR-
Your Relationship to Money

---

*"Waiting for circumstances to change so you can feel good
is like looking in a mirror waiting for your
reflection to smile first."*
—Bashar

"I don't want to have to think about money. I don't want to have to deal with it at all. I just want it to be there."

Every time I hear that from a client, and I hear it a lot, I feel a little badly for money. What an interesting, and problematic, relationship that is to money—as though it is a nuisance and a bothersome pain in the neck. A chore. A burden.

Imagine you are advertising for a relationship and you wrote this ad:

"I don't want to have to pay attention to you. I don't want to have to think about you or deal with you in any way. I just want you to be there for me when I need you. Send photo."

Who would sign up for that? It is not attractive energy.

Over the years I have encountered many un-useful ways of relating to money.

In addition to **The Nuisance**—described above—I have noticed some other common ways of relating to money.

The Angry Adolescent - This energy is angry, righteous and entitled. As though life owes them something and life hasn't delivered. Imagine writing this advertisement for a relationship: "Where the #@*% are you? I've been waiting for you to *#@& show up. You owe me. Send **recent** @%#* photo."

The Desperate Supplicant - This energy is powerless and pleading. "Please let me win the lottery, please, please, please." This ad would go something like, "Please save me. Please help me. I can't do it on my own. I'll be good, I promise. Please rescue me. Please." (I actually do know people who would answer that ad, but it's not the basis for an ideal relationship.)

The Superior Being*- This energy is aloof and superior. It goes something like this, "I am not interested in anything as base/crass/materialistic as money. I am a spiritual person. I am interested in more important things." This ad would read, "I am not interested in you. You are not important. I am interested in more important things than you. I am better than you. In fact, don't bother to reply." *(Before doing Money Magic I had a bad case of this one, so I know it well, and a lot of people who hold themselves as intellectuals or spiritual can fall into this category.)

The Unworthy Worm - This is pretty much just like it sounds. (And although it seems like the opposite of the Superior Being, they actually both come from similar shaky foundations and lack of right to exist. (I would say more, but that's a whole other book.) This ad would sound more like, "I know I don't deserve you. I know you have better places to be and better things to do. I'm not worth your time and attention. I know you won't respond. Sorry for taking up your time."

The way you relate to money is at the core of your money experience. The way you relate to money is a projection of your beliefs and family patterns onto money.

When creating Money Magic, I wanted to find a way to reveal people's subconscious relationship to money, and then revise it if necessary. So, I took a change pattern created by Fritz Perls called Perceptual Positions and adapted it to money—adding in a little Family Constellation work as well. (This change pattern is included at the end of this chapter.)

One of the interesting things that have come from doing this over and over with workshop participants is that we have discovered that when all of the family stuff that is projected onto money is removed, money always shows up with the same energy.

The pure energy of money shows up as warm, benevolent, and unattached.

It is the energy of blessings.

It is supportive and nurturing and available. We have seen this consistently in workshops. It feels like money is one of the many ways the universe wants to love us. So much of what is projected onto money has nothing to do with money.

Once at a workshop, after demonstrating this exercise with one woman who originally felt disconnected from money, one of the watching participants said that he didn't understand what her problem was. He said, "I would just run and grab money. So, I have no problem with money, right?"

I had him come up and sit in the chair across from money and asked him what that was like. He sat on the edge of his seat and said he wanted to go grab it.

Then I asked him to imagine that in the chair, instead of money, was the energy of blessings. "Oh," he said, sitting back in his chair, "that's different." I asked him how that felt. "Much calmer," he said. Until he'd had that experience, he had confused fear and desperation with enthusiasm.

One of the common themes that shows up when doing this exercise is a sense of disconnection with money. In those cases, there is almost always a disconnection from one or both parents. When that shows up, I will often ask someone, "Who in your family was it difficult to connect with?" or "Who does that energy remind you of?" Then we get another chair to represent that person and place it near the money chair and take all of that person's energy out of money and then put it in the new chair. Then we let the participant experience themselves, money and their relationship to money without the family member's energy mixed in. (Sometimes there are generations of people's energies mixed in. You need a lot of chairs then. We will cover the effect of previous generations in the next chapter.)

What I am about to share with you is a stunningly simple exercise but incredibly powerful. (It is so simple and powerful that since I started demonstrating it, it has spread like wildfire through the coaching and personal development world.) It is so quick and so revealing, that I still do it myself every six months or so, to check on my relationship to money. (All the change patterns in Money Magic can be repeated periodically. Just doing them once in your life is like getting the oil in your car changed once-or only getting it serviced once, or only getting your teeth cleaned once. You get the idea.)

So, now it's time to find out what relationship you have been projecting onto money.

Change Pattern: Relating to Money

This is an adaptation of Fritz Perls' Perceptual Positions, with some family systems work layered in.

Set up three chairs. Place two of them across from each other, and the third equidistant between the two but set back a bit removed.

#3 Observer

#1 You   #2 Money

Sit down in Chair #1. Look across at Chair #2 and imagine the energy of Money there.

Notice what your attitude and energy toward it is. How does it feel? Do you feel connected? Once you have noticed what it's like for you to relate to money, leave all of that in the chair and get up.

Then go and sit down in Chair #2, into Money's point of view, and see yourself sitting across in Chair #1.

Notice what it's like to be in the energy of Money. What is Money's energy like? Then notice the energy coming off the person in Chair #1. What is their energy like? Does it feel like there is a connection between you?

Now get up and sit down in Chair #3. Notice the "you" in Chair #1 and the energy of Money in Chair #2.

Notice the energy between them.

Finally, get up and sit back down in Chair #1, but this time with any added perspectives you may have gained from the other positions. Notice if, and how, your energy and attitudes toward money may have shifted.

(If the energy of money showed up with any energy or attitude other than warm and benevolent, take a moment to notice whose energy in your family is that attitude like? It is often a parent or grandparent.

Then get a separate chair to represent that person(s) and place it beside the Money chair.

Sit in the Money chair and feel all of that family member's energy, and then stand up, taking all of their energy with you and sit down in the new chair.

Let their energy have its own chair separate from Money.

Then sit back down in your chair and notice what Money's energy is like when the family energy is no longer mixed in. Notice the difference between the energy of Money and the energy of your family.

Say to Money, "I have been confusing you with the energy of my family. You are not my family. You are money."

Then go through the exercise one more time, without the family energy mixed into Money's energy.)

CHAPTER SEVEN

The Biggest Block to Everything You Want

-OR-

God Must Really Love Rap Musicians

"There's no vocabulary
For love within a family, love that's lived in
But not looked at, love within the light of which
All else is seen, the love within which
All other love finds speech.
This love is silent."
—T.S. Eliot

The Day the Cool Died

I remember the day the last shreds of any delusions I may have had that I was cool, died. I was in a car with my 15-year-old stepdaughter and her friend, and I was playing music. I was playing my more recent purchases, (Usher, Missy Elliot, Duffy, etc.) and they were singing along. I was feeling pretty good about all this until one of them turned to the other and said, "I really like listening to these oldies. It makes me feel nostalgic." The car kept moving, but my coolness came to a screeching halt and died right there on the 680 freeway, somewhere between Walnut Creek and Pleasant Hill.

Despite that ship having sailed, I would still watch music awards shows on television however, and I noticed an interesting thing happened with surprising frequency, especially in the Rap categories. Someone would win an award, often for a song that sounded fairly dark and violent, and when they accepted the award they would say something like, "I'd like to thank our Lord and savior Jesus Christ for the success *of #@*% the #$@* with a %$#*^*. He has a plan for *#@*% the #$@* with a %$#*^*, and we're gonna make it happen." Rap musicians seemed to be the new chosen people. (I actually mean no disrespect to *#@*% the #$@* with a %$#*^* or the men who sang it, or Rap musicians. It was just that the juxtaposition of someone who is usually associated with peace and gentle compassion against the violent sound of the song caught me by surprise.)

I actually have no doubt that God, or Jesus, or the Universe does love those artists completely, and wants the best for them. The mission part, however, especially caught my attention. It's possible that believing that they have a mission is a big part of how they can allow, and justify, success.

This brings us to the last, and **biggest block to everything** you want.

Subconscious Family Loyalties

Imagine if you were really hungry, and in front of you was a plate of your favorite food, but all around you were hundreds of your family members and ancestors—none of whom have any food. How okay would it feel to go ahead and happily eat to your heart's content? In a case like that, most people would try to stretch their plate of food to give everyone a molecule of it, or give it away, or push their food away altogether and just not eat. At a restaurant, even when we know our other party members' food is coming, most of us will wait until everyone is served before we start to eat. As humans, it feels wrong to have it better than the people we come from, or the people we are with.

So, if someone from a family or community that is poor, or impoverished, makes a lot of money, they can often feel guilty for having it, when others don't. And when they feel guilty, they may either get the money to go away (subconsciously sabotaging themselves), or, they may try to find a way to justify having it (by having it "I can help others," "spread the word," "be an example.")

This awareness first began for me in 1996 when I read a 2-page article in a magazine that talked about the revolutionary work of a man named Bert Hellinger. His work was said to reveal deep, generational blocks in our lives. I explored this with a group I was working with at the time and was stunned at the profound dynamics that were uncovered. After that, I read every book of Bert Hellinger's that I found, watched every video, and attended every training of his that I could when he came to the San Francisco Bay area. Bert Hellinger had taken something called Family Constellations, which Virginia Satir (the famous author and psychotherapist) had been doing, and he evolved it and noticed some profound dynamics operating in families *across generations*. He called these subconscious loyalties "entanglements."

In the more than 20 years that I have been working with people, I have noticed that when blocks won't shift for someone, no matter what they or I do, it's because there are one or more of these subconscious entanglements, or loyalties, running.

Bert Hellinger noticed that one of the primary drives behind these entanglements is the drive to belong. People will do almost anything to belong. People will die to belong—otherwise, war would not be possible. And, unfortunately, we usually compute our belonging in its crudest form—i.e., in terms of conformity. If we are like the people we come from, we feel like we belong, and we feel innocent. If we feel like we are different from the people we come from, then we often feel like we don't belong. When we suffer with or like, the people we come from, we feel like we belong. When we have a better experience than them, our belonging feels threatened, and we feel guilty. And these feelings of guilt and innocence are not about right and wrong—they are about belonging.

Bert Hellinger famously said, "In a family of thieves, a child who does not steal, feels guilty."

In a family or community, of people who don't have money, someone who does have money is likely to feel guilty. And when we feel guilty, there is a strong inclination to get rid of the money, or suffer in some other way, so that we can feel innocent (and like we belong) again.

There are two main ways I see this playing out for people. The first is them limiting their finances to be like the people they come from.

An example of this first dynamic is a woman who told me that every time she starts to do well in her business, she will attract a "dragon lady"—someone who will really "crack the whip." In fact, when she used the phrase "crack the whip," she made a gesture of someone cracking a whip. It was strikingly intense when she did it. Later, when we were talking about her family history, it turned out that she was directly descended from slaves. So, when she would start to do well (i.e., have a much better, richer life than her slave

MONEY MAGIC

ancestors), she would subconsciously attract a replay of a slave owner to put her in her place.

Another example is a client of mine who said he felt compelled to "be a failure." When I asked him who in his family was a failure, he was surprised and momentarily taken aback. Then a light dawned in his eyes, and he said, "My father." His father's business had failed, and he had never recovered from it. My client was subconsciously trying to fail, to be like his father, and not do better than his father.

Yet another client would get very fearful any time he started to make money. He told me, "It's not safe to be noticed." He was Jewish, and the major part of his mother's family had been wiped out in the Holocaust. Since it wasn't safe for them to be noticed, he was entangled with their fears and fate.

The second main way these loyalties can affect people is in causing them to get rid of money if their family accumulated wealth improperly, or, benefitted from someone else's loss or misfortune.

For instance, a man came to see me once for his gambling problem. He said to me, "It's like I'm trying to lose my house." When he said that a bell went off in my head, and I wondered to myself, "Who was it that lost a house?" When we started talking about his family history, he told me that his family had moved from Mexico to just outside Los Angeles in the early 1900s. His family had a little farm next to a Japanese family. After Pearl Harbor, in 1942, when Japanese Americans were put in internment camps, his family got the neighboring Japanese family's house. His family benefited from the Japanese family's loss, and so the family carried a subconscious guilt, which he was trying to repay by losing his house.

Another example is a wonderful and talented man (ethnically Chinese) who came to do work with me because he just wouldn't let himself make or keep much money. His grandfather was a developer and contractor in Malaysia during the time of the people's revolution in China and owned a portfolio of businesses in the construction and resources industries. He was also donating many profits to Chiang Kai Shek who at the time, was being pushed out of China and was forming what is now known as Taiwan.

My client's father's role in the grandfather's company was to identify and "remove" undercover communists within the organization. He said, "The company did great things but also a bunch of not so great things...and, in my system, money was entangled by a whole hairball of terrifying projections and destructive energies. As a result, the undistorted glorious and true nature of money wasn't something my system had access to."

If the people we come from have struggled with money, or have not had a lot of it, or have profited from another's loss and misery, we often will not let ourselves have it, or keep it.

This instinctive compunction to suffer with, or like, the people we come from is beautifully loving and human, but it is also futile and destructive. Nothing that we do to ourselves, no amount of limitation or struggle, makes anything better for the people we come from. And nothing that we do to ourselves, rights any wrongs that our family committed in the past. It just adds more suffering and limitation to the world.

A channel named Jason and the Nine summed this up quite poetically. He (they) said, *"When you join someone in their suffering, all you do is make more suffering."*

And each generation that limits their happiness, well-being and wealth out of love and loyalty to the people they come from, limits how much things can get better for everyone in the present, and, puts pressure on future generations to not have it too much better either.

MONEY MAGIC

We can all notice that an eye for an eye and a tooth for a tooth leaves the world blind and toothless but joining people in their suffering also makes more suffering in the world—even though it is done from a place of love rather than revenge. The end result is still more suffering.

No matter how much we may want to, we cannot undo the pain and tragedies of the past. We can't carry the burdens on our forbearers' hearts or heal our parents' pain. And if we try, all we end up doing is replicating their pain and burdens, not healing or carrying them. You can't carry someone else's pain, any more than you can carry their constipation. You can't take medicine for someone else if they are sick. You can't eat for someone else or go to therapy for them. There is nothing harder than seeing, hearing or feeling the people we love be in pain, but when we re-create their pain out of love and loyalty, we just make more pain. And no one benefits from creating more pain in the world. Everyone who makes a choice not to suffer contributes to the forwarding of humanity.

There are better ways for us to express our love and belonging with the people we come from than through replaying their struggles and limiting our own well-being.

Every life has its' own unique path and challenges. *It's not for us to judge or fix the paths of those who came before us.* The only path any of us have any authority over is our own (and if we are parents, we briefly have some influence over our children's lives). Each generation has its own unique challenges and opportunities, and it is there where we can make a difference—in the present and future.

And so, toward that end, find a place where you can sit comfortably as you do the following piece.

Change pattern: Releasing Ancestral Suffering Visualization.

Take a moment to look at the family tree diagram.

You

Parents (2)

Grandparents (4)

Great Grandparents (8)

Great Great Grandparents (16)

Great Great Great Grandparents (32)

MONEY MAGIC

In your mind's eye, notice all the people who came before you—parents, aunts and uncles, grandparents, great aunts and uncles, great grandparents and their siblings, and all those who came before them, stretching out like an infinite triangle reaching into the past, with you at the apex. Many of those who came before, had lives of difficulty, struggle and loss. War, famine, poverty, oppression, persecution, scarcity and lack were present in all cultures. For many, there was barely enough. You cannot help them or undo their struggles and losses. If you join them in their suffering, all you do is create more suffering. With love and respect, you *must leave their challenges and burdens with them.*

If you have children, notice that if you suffer like those who came before you, it doesn't help them—all it does is bring their pain and suffering into the present, instead of *letting it end.* It brings the suffering closer to your children and descendants. You cannot save those who came before you, but you can help those who come after you if you *let the suffering end.* When you try to make it better for those who came before, all you do is make it harder for those who come after. With love and respect, you must *leave the challenges and burdens of the past in the past.*

All families have potentials for joy, happiness, love and creativity. In some families those potentials have not gotten a chance to flower—they have remained closed in a bud state or only opened partially, depriving the family and others of really experiencing the family's potential. As someone who carries the accumulated gifts and potentials of thousands of generations, you can *let go of the family's pain and suffering.* Then *the family's potential for joy, happiness, creativity and love may blossom in the world.* In you, the gifts of your family can finally express and contribute to the world. The gifts and potentials of you and your ancestors become the bedrock for your descendants (if you have them), and others, to build on.

Now address your ancestors and in the privacy of your own mind and heart say to them, "*In the past, there were many struggles. Sometimes there was sometimes barely enough to survive. But the family has endured and continued. It is a different time now. The struggles of the past are not the challenges of the future. **There can be more than enough now.** Our family can **begin to thrive.** I love you with my whole heart, and I always will. I wish you all great joy, happiness and peace. I honor your struggles and challenges as yours, and I leave them, and the dignity of those challenges, with you. I will not add to the burdens you carried by re-creating your suffering, misery, sadness, pain and loss. Instead, **I will take the gifts and potentials I received from you and give them a good home.** The strength and dignity you gained from your struggles, as well as your gifts and potentials shall be your legacy in my life—not the pain and loss. The best of all of you lives in every cell of my body. Your strength, gifts, talents and potentials will be welcome in my life. I will share them, and the best of you with the world and those I love. Please lend me your support and blessings as I begin a new chapter for myself and our family.*"

Allow a symbol to arise to represent the family potential and blessings. Take that symbol into your heart where it can flourish.

Now, notice that attention is like water—causing experiences to grow in depth and magnitude. Rather than feeding the sufferings of the past, honor them for what they were, and what they cost, and then, with respect, **withdraw your attention from the pain and suffering of the past**, so that the suffering can fade and finish, and **pour your attention into the strengths and gifts of your family across time, past, present and into the future**, so that *those gifts and strengths may grow and thrive*. Feel your family's unique strengths and gifts flowing down into you, adding to your own. Feel the weight and power of that great river of potential and abilities behind you, flowing to you and through you out into your life and future. Feel your part in moving the family forward toward a greater expression of love, freedom, choice and abundance. *Allow that to continue to strengthen and deepen* in just those ways, and just those times that most fully support the integration of these awarenesses into your heart and mind and soul, out into your everyday interactions and behaviors, and into an ever-increasing experience of freedom and choice in life and well-being.

As that continues throughout the deeper levels of your being, you can begin to bring your attention back at your own pace to the present.

CHAPTER EIGHT

The Death of the Zero Sum
-OR-

How Many Jelly Beans in the Universal Jar?

"You Are Not a Drop in the Ocean; You Are the Entire Ocean in a Drop."
—Rumi

How Many Jelly Beans in the Jar?

One of the most common misconceptions about money is that there is a fixed quantifiable amount of it in the world and that the portion that one person or persons takes from it decreases the amount available for everyone else.

This is zero-sum thinking.

Zero-sum thinking basically says that if there are 100 jelly beans in the jar, and one person takes 20 jelly beans (which by the way shows remarkable restraint), then that means there are only 80 jelly beans left for everyone else.

This is the subconscious model most people apply to the world money supply.

First of all, it presupposes a fixed quantifiable amount of money in the world.

Secondly, it presupposes that what one person takes from the universal money pool decreases the amount available for everyone else.

Starting with the first notion, i.e., that there is a fixed quantifiable amount of money in the world, let's notice that before there was money, there was barter. Barter was a direct exchange of items of value or services for other items of value or services. If Olaf had eggs and you had pickles, and you wanted eggs, then you could give Olaf some pickles for his eggs. Then everybody had something to bring to a picnic.

Physical money eventually evolved as an abstraction of value that could be exchanged for almost anything. If you wanted eggs, but Olaf didn't want your pickles, then you could give him physical money for the eggs which he could exchange for whatever he did want—cabbage maybe. This saved Olaf from having to find a cabbage vendor who either wanted eggs or pickles, and made exchange much more open-ended. Physical money has come in many forms—shells, beads, paper and precious metals are some of the most common. In some cultures, dowries are paid in goats. A hundred-goat bride is nothing to sneeze at.

In Western culture, until fairly recently, money was based on precious metals. The United States used the gold standard; the British pound was based on silver, etc. Historically, a British pound note was worth the equivalent of a pound of sterling silver. In 1834, a new U.S. dollar was backed by 1.50 g of gold. And so on.

MONEY MAGIC

This is no longer true anymore. Governments routinely print paper money that's not based on any physical commodity. The value of the U.S. dollar now is based on a collective belief and hallucination in the stability and weight of the United States. When it comes down to how much money there is in the world, nobody really knows. It is continually changing. Money has become an abstraction for exchange of value.

How much value is there in the world? No one knows. Value is continually changing, emerging, receding, etc. Value is in the eyes of the beholder, and the beholders are continually changing. *There is no fixed amount of money or value in the world.*

In her one-woman play *The Search for Intelligent Life in the Universe* (written by Jane Wagner), Lily Tomlin says that reality is just a collective hunch. The same could be said of money.

A woman who was getting ready to retire once listened to a recording from the first morning of a Money Magic workshop. "That was nice," she said. A week or two later she was called to have a meeting with a representative from Social Security. The representative discovered, much to the surprise of the woman, that she was eligible for an additional benefit she didn't know about, which gave her enough extra each month to live more comfortably. Then just as she was getting ready to retire, her boss informed her that the business was closing down—allowing her to qualify for unemployment. Her "fixed income" had suddenly expanded.

The Expansive Sum

Money is just a collective hunch. Or more precisely, money is a concept—an idea. And nobody knows how many ideas there are in the world. Because ideas, and value, are limitless.

This brings us to the second notion—that the amount of money one person has detracts from the amount available for everyone else.

Since there is not a finite pool of value in the world, what one person receives does not diminish what is available for anyone else. In fact, more ideas and more value, tend to beget even more ideas and more value. The pool of ideas expands. The more people who let themselves be healthy, the more health there is. The more people who let themselves be happy, the more happiness there is. The amount of health, happiness, and value *expands*.

Here are some analogies to make this a little clearer:

If you stand in the sunlight, do you make the world darker for everyone else?

If you have an idea, do you take away ideas from anyone else?

If you sing a song, do you take that song away from anyone else?

If you have a child, do you take away anyone else's ability to have a child?

If you have been really healthy, do you decide to be sick for a while so as to not use up all the well-being in the world? (This one is from the magnificent Esther/Abraham Hicks.)

If you become inspired and happy, does someone else have to become more miserable and depressed?

Happiness, health, wealth and well-being are not zero-sum realities.

In fact, it is quite the opposite.

Health, wealth, and happiness are expansive sums. We just keep adding to what's possible.

The better it gets for any, the better it gets for all.

CHAPTER NINE

You Walk in Magic
-OR-
Your Greatest Symphony of All

"Out beyond ideas of wrongdoing and rightdoing
there is a field. I'll meet you there."
—Rumi

A long time ago, I read a Navajo prayer in a book somewhere that I have found to be very inspiring. I remember it reading something like,

"Beauty behind me
Beauty before me
Beauty above me
Beauty below me
Beauty to the left of me
Beauty to the right of me
Beauty within me
Beauty all around me
I walk in Beauty"

It is such a lovely prayer.

I remember hearing someone discounting something beautiful at Walt Disney World once by saying, "Yeah, but it's not real. It's just a fantasy." It struck me as so odd at the time. This person was asserting that poverty and crime were "real" and this Disney creation was "fantasy." It seemed odd to me because crime, poverty, war, etc., are also creations—consciously or not, we create all those things we call "real." So, since it is all a creation, why not create something beautiful? Why is the sweet, imaginative architecture in Fantasyland any less real than an ugly tenement apartment building? Things that are "gritty," are no more real than things that are wonderful--they are just harder and darker.

Why are stories of war and strife any more "real" than stories of love and inspiration and friendship?

We make it all up. We create it all.

Now that we are learning this, we can *begin to create* it *more and more from places of inspiration, possibility and beauty*, rather than fear.

A friend of mine took a photography class where the homework one week was to take two portrait shots of someone one right after the other—just seconds apart. Just before they clicked the shutter button of one, they were supposed to notice all the "flaws" of the subject's face. Then they were to take a second picture of the same person, but this time just before they clicked the shutter button they were supposed to notice all that was beautiful and unique about the subject's face. Nothing else was different—no changes of angle, lighting, position—it was just a change in the **mental** filter they were using.

My friend said the results were astonishing—the differences were so huge. No one had to ask anyone which mental filter the photographer was using in each case. It was stunningly obvious. This was "beauty is in the eye of the beholder" at a quantum level.

We create our lives at every level, so why not create from joy and beauty? Why not create abundance and satisfaction? A slide projector requires no more energy to project a beautiful image than an ugly one. The same is true of universal consciousness.

It takes no more energy to create beauty, wealth, health and happiness than to create strife, struggle and lack.

We have been projecting old images, often based in fear and lack, onto the quantum mind space. As we clear up the old patterns and fears that created those images, we have the opportunity to *project something new and beautiful.*

You may have noticed that there are three quotes from Rumi in this book. That's no accident. Rumi's work was fueled by joy and inspiration. His work is sublime.

I heard once that Beethoven's final symphony, the *Ninth Symphony*, "The Ode to Joy," took as long for him to write as all the previous eight symphonies combined. It is his masterwork—the sum of it all.

There's been enough pain and lack and struggle. It's time for your masterwork.

Joy is a masterwork. And it is sublime.

Hafez said, "Stay close to anything that makes you glad you are alive."

And so, one last story, because if fear is contagious, so are joy, inspiration and appreciation.

One participant who had taken Money Magic had come from a very poor background. There were many children, and never any money for extras—things like new clothes were impossible then. So, after the workshop, when she started making a lot more money, she went to Banana Republic, got a personal shopper, and bought herself a whole new wardrobe. Then she did the same for her mother. It was so meaningful for her, in fact, that she wrote a letter to the store and the personal shopper thanking them. She said what it had been like growing up, and what it meant to her now that she could do this. The letter was so impactful that the store began sharing it with other stores. Then the company printed it in their newsletter. What was so meaningful for her, became meaningful for the whole company. The ripples of her change and appreciation spread out in ways she could never have imagined.

This is true for each of us.

The better it gets for each of us, the bigger the ripples of joy, satisfaction and possibility that we spread.

And so, in closing, I would like to offer another version of that Navajo prayer to keep in mind.

Magic behind you
Magic before you
Magic above you
Magic below you
Magic to the left of you
Magic to the right of you
Magic within you
Magic all around you
You walk in Magic

May you walk in Beauty, Joy and Magic,

—Michelle

Want More Magic?

If you would like to delve further into this work, you might consider coming to one of our live or online workshops. This work is always evolving and expanding. Money Magic Live and Online Money Magic include all of the exercises in the book plus many more, and they create their own unique energy.

In addition to Money Magic, we offer other transformational workshops, such as Clear Path to Love, The Field of Money, and a one-day adoption workshop. Trainings in NLP, using Metaphors for Change, and Family Systems for Coaches are some of the other trainings we offer, schedule permitting.

To find out more go to www.michellemastersnlp.com or send an email to info@michellemastersnlp.com

ACKNOWLEDGEMENTS

"If I have seen further than others,
it is by standing upon the shoulders of giants."
—Isaac Newton

I don't know that I have seen further than anyone, but my dusty, pronated footprints are definitely all over the shoulders of many.

I am deeply thankful for the founders of NLP (Neuro-Linguistic Programming) John Grinder, Richard Bandler (and many others) and for the genius of the people they modeled: Virginia Satir, Fritz Perls, and Milton Erickson especially.

I am also greatly appreciative of the people I have learned from directly and indirectly: Jonathan Rice, Andrea Stallsworth Rice, David Gordon, Michael Banks, Steve and Connirae Andreas, Robert Dilts, Bert Hellinger, Hunter Beaumont, John Overdorf, Richard Bartlett, and Melissa Joy.

After a twelve year gestation, a big thank you also to Jon, Hilary, Ashley and Trevor at Epic Author Publishing for their expertise and wisdom in finally helping me get this book delivered with a minimum of crying and hyperventilating.

My mother and father gave me life, and gifts beyond counting, especially my mother, who found a way to raise a child alone and send me to college.

Then there's my partner, Jade, who made life a place I really want to be, and the world a place I really want to see.

This book truly would not exist if it weren't for the two founders of NLP Marin: Bob Hoffmeyer and Carl Buchheit. Bob Hoffmeyer was a businessman with such wisdom, heart and integrity that the foundation he set for NLP Marin in 1993 still exists today. The thousands of us who have benefited from the work at NLP Marin owe him so much, and I am so thankful to have met him.

Finally, there's Carl Buchheit, the founding Trainer of NLP Marin. I am sometimes standing on his shoulders, sometimes hanging on to his pant leg, and sometimes running to keep up with him. Anyone who has met Carl can see that he is brilliant, funny, kind and exceedingly generous. But the things I learned from him, and the private sessions he did with me, transformed my life and my sense of self in ways I could never have dreamed of. I didn't realize how badly I had felt until life got better. My worst days now are better than my best days used to be. Life is now the magical place I always hoped it would be. If a lot of what is in my writing sounds like Carl, it's because I soaked up his wisdom and teaching in more ways than I can tell, and I am so very thankful for him.

ABOUT THE AUTHOR

Michelle Masters has been a teacher, speaker and transformational facilitator since 1996. She is based in the U.S. but works with people all over the world in live workshops, or online in groups, and private sessions. Her work combines a unique mixture of neuro-based change patterns, family constellation work and quantum healing modalities in a fun, easy and inspiring way. The work she does with people is designed to create deep, lasting change without having to struggle or try to be different.

When not teaching abroad, Michelle lives in Northern California with her partner and family, where she grows an inordinate amount of tomatoes.

To find out more about Michelle and her work go to: www.michellemastersnlp.com

Printed in Great Britain
by Amazon